Jumpstarters for the U.S. Constitution

Short ~~D~~ ~~m~~-ups for the Classroom

By
CINDY BARDEN

~~COPY~~RIGHT © 2005 Mark Twain Media, Inc.

~~ISB~~N 10-digit: 1-58037-304-6
        13-digit: 978-1-58037-304-3

Printing No. CD-404031

Mark Twain Media, Inc., Publishers
Distributed by Carson-Dellosa Publishing LLC

Visit us at www.carsondellosa.com

Table of Contents

Introduction to Parents and Teachers

Warm-ups help students prepare for the day's lesson while reviewing what they have previously learned. Part of being a good citizen involves understanding our government and how it works. To do this, students need to understand our most important document: the Constitution of the United States.

The short warm-up activities presented in this book, *Jumpstarters for the U.S. Constitution*, provide activities to help students learn more about the U.S. Constitution through the use of a dictionary, a variety of other reference sources, and original-source material.

Each student should have a copy of the Constitution so he or she can read, add personal notes to, and highlight important points. A copy of the Constitution follows this page. The original spelling and capitalization have been retained in this copy. Changes made to the Constitution by amendments are noted in italics.

Each activity page contains five warm-ups—one for each day of the week. Used at the beginning of class, warm-ups help students focus on an aspect of the Constitution they have previously read and/or discussed in class. Students are encouraged to think about what they read, form opinions, answer questions, compare and contrast, write pros and cons on issues, and differentiate between facts and opinions. Periodic reviews are also included.

Suggestions for using warm-up activities:

- Copy and cut apart one page each week. Give students one warm-up activity each day at the beginning of class.

- Give each student a copy of the entire page to complete day by day. Students can keep the completed pages in a three-ring binder to use as a resource for review.

- Make transparencies of individual warm-ups and complete the activities as a group.

Useful websites:

http://www.archives.gov/exhibits/charters/constitution_transcript.html

http://www.house.gov/content/learn

Age-appropriate sources of information and background on the U.S. Constitution:

Creating the Constitution (The Drama of American History series) by Christopher and James Lincoln Collier.

Understanding the U.S. Constitution by Mark A. Stange.

The U.S. Constitution and You by Syl Sobel.

U.S. Constitution: Preparing for the Test by George Lee.

The Constitution of the United States

Preamble

We the People of the United States, in Order to form a more perfect Union, establish Justice, insure domestic Tranquility, provide for the common defence, promote the general Welfare, and secure the Blessings of Liberty to ourselves and our Posterity, do ordain and establish this Constitution for the United States of America.

Article I. - The Legislative Branch
Section 1 - The Legislature

All legislative Powers herein granted shall be vested in a Congress of the United States, which shall consist of a Senate and House of Representatives.

Section 2 - The House

The House of Representatives shall be composed of Members chosen every second Year by the People of the several States, and the Electors in each State shall have the Qualifications requisite for Electors of the most numerous Branch of the State Legislature.

No Person shall be a Representative who shall not have attained to the Age of twenty-five Years, and been seven Years a Citizen of the United States, and who shall not, when elected, be an Inhabitant of that State in which he shall be chosen.

Representatives and direct Taxes shall be apportioned among the several States which may be included within this Union, according to their respective Numbers, [which shall be determined by adding to the whole Number of free Persons, including those bound to Service for a Term of Years, and excluding Indians not taxed, three-fifths of all other Persons.] *Note: Amendment XIV, Section 2 replaced the sentence in brackets.*

The actual Enumeration shall be made within three Years after the first Meeting of the Congress of the United States, and within every subsequent Term of ten Years, in such Manner as they shall by Law direct. The Number of Representatives shall not exceed one for every thirty Thousand, but each State shall have at Least one Representative; and until such enumeration shall be made, the State of New Hampshire shall be entitled to chuse three, Massachusetts eight, Rhode Island and Providence Plantations one, Connecticut five, New York six, New Jersey four, Pennsylvania eight, Delaware one, Maryland six, Virginia ten, North Carolina five, South Carolina five, and Georgia three.

When vacancies happen in the Representation from any State, the Executive Authority thereof shall issue Writs of Election to fill such Vacancies. The House of Representatives shall chuse their Speaker and other Officers, and shall have the sole Power of Impeachment.

Section 3 - The Senate

The Senate of the United States shall be composed of two Senators from each State, [chosen by the Legislature thereof,] *Note: Amendment XVII, Section 1 changed the words in brackets.* for six Years; and each Senator shall have one Vote.

The Constitution of the United States (cont.)

Immediately after they shall be assembled in Consequence of the first Election, they shall be divided as equally as may be into three Classes. The Seats of the Senators of the first Class shall be vacated at the Expiration of the second Year, of the second Class at the Expiration of the fourth Year, and of the third Class at the Expiration of the sixth Year, so that one-third may be chosen every second Year; [and if Vacancies happen by Resignation, or otherwise, during the Recess of the Legislature of any State, the Executive thereof may make temporary Appointments until the next Meeting of the Legislature, which shall then fill such Vacancies.] *Note: Amendment XVII, Section 2 changed the words in brackets.*

No person shall be a Senator who shall not have attained to the Age of thirty Years, and been nine Years a Citizen of the United States, and who shall not, when elected, be an Inhabitant of that State for which he shall be chosen. The Vice President of the United States shall be President of the Senate, but shall have no Vote, unless they be equally divided.

The Senate shall chuse their other Officers, and also a President pro tempore, in the absence of the Vice President, or when he shall exercise the Office of President of the United States. The Senate shall have the sole Power to try all Impeachments. When sitting for that Purpose, they shall be on Oath or Affirmation. When the President of the United States is tried, the Chief Justice shall preside: And no Person shall be convicted without the Concurrence of two-thirds of the Members present.

Judgment in Cases of Impeachment shall not extend further than to removal from Office, and disqualification to hold and enjoy any Office of honor, Trust or Profit under the United States: but the Party convicted shall nevertheless be liable and subject to Indictment, Trial, Judgment and Punishment, according to Law.

Section 4 - Elections, Meetings
The Times, Places and Manner of holding Elections for Senators and Representatives, shall be prescribed in each State by the Legislature thereof; but the Congress may at any time by Law make or alter such Regulations, except as to the Place of Chusing Senators.

The Congress shall assemble at least once in every Year, and such Meeting shall be on [the first Monday in December] unless they shall by Law appoint a different Day. *Note: Amendment XX, Section 2 changed the words in brackets.*

Section 5 - Membership, Rules, Journals, Adjournment
Each House shall be the Judge of the Elections, Returns and Qualifications of its own Members, and a Majority of each shall constitute a Quorum to do Business; but a smaller number may adjourn from day to day, and may be authorized to compel the Attendance of absent Members, in such Manner, and under such Penalties as each House may provide.

The Constitution of the United States (cont.)

Each House may determine the Rules of its Proceedings, punish its Members for disorderly Behavior, and, with the Concurrence of two-thirds, expel a Member. Each House shall keep a Journal of its Proceedings, and from time to time publish the same, excepting such Parts as may in their Judgment require Secrecy; and the Yeas and Nays of the Members of either House on any question shall, at the Desire of one-fifth of those Present, be entered on the Journal.

Neither House, during the Session of Congress, shall, without the Consent of the other, adjourn for more than three days, nor to any other Place than that in which the two Houses shall be sitting.

Section 6 - Compensation

[The Senators and Representatives shall receive a Compensation for their Services, to be ascertained by Law, and paid out of the Treasury of the United States.] *Note: Amendment XXVII modified the words in brackets.*

They shall in all Cases, except Treason, Felony and Breach of the Peace, be privileged from Arrest during their Attendance at the Session of their respective Houses, and in going to and returning from the same; and for any Speech or Debate in either House, they shall not be questioned in any other Place.

No Senator or Representative shall, during the Time for which he was elected, be appointed to any civil Office under the Authority of the United States which shall have been created, or the Emoluments whereof shall have been increased during such time; and no Person holding any Office under the United States, shall be a Member of either House during his Continuance in Office.

Section 7 - Revenue Bills, Legislative Process, Presidential Veto

All bills for raising Revenue shall originate in the House of Representatives; but the Senate may propose or concur with Amendments as on other Bills. Every Bill which shall have passed the House of Representatives and the Senate, shall, before it becomes a Law, be presented to the President of the United States; if he approve he shall sign it, but if not he shall return it, with his Objections to that House in which it shall have originated, who shall enter the Objections at large on their Journal, and proceed to reconsider it. If after such Reconsideration two-thirds of that House shall agree to pass the Bill, it shall be sent, together with the Objections, to the other House, by which it shall likewise be reconsidered, and if approved by two-thirds of that House, it shall become a Law. But in all such Cases the Votes of both Houses shall be determined by Yeas and Nays, and the Names of the Persons voting for and against the Bill shall be entered on the Journal of each House respectively. If any Bill shall not be returned by the President within ten Days (Sundays excepted) after it shall have been presented to him, the Same shall be a Law, in like Manner as if he had signed it, unless the Congress by their Adjournment prevent its Return, in which Case it shall not be a Law.

The Constitution of the United States (cont.)

Every Order, Resolution, or Vote to which the Concurrence of the Senate and House of Representatives may be necessary (except on a question of Adjournment) shall be presented to the President of the United States; and before the Same shall take Effect, shall be approved by him, or being disapproved by him, shall be repassed by two-thirds of the Senate and House of Representatives, according to the Rules and Limitations prescribed in the Case of a Bill.

Section 8 - Powers of Congress

The Congress shall have Power To lay and collect Taxes, Duties, Imposts, and Excises, to pay the Debts and provide for the common Defence and general Welfare of the United States; but all Duties, Imposts and Excises shall be uniform throughout the United States;

To borrow money on the credit of the United States;

To regulate Commerce with foreign Nations, and among the several States, and with the Indian Tribes;

To establish a uniform Rule of Naturalization, and uniform Laws on the subject of Bankruptcies throughout the United States;

To coin Money, regulate the Value thereof, and of foreign Coin, and fix the Standard of Weights and Measures;

To provide for the Punishment of counterfeiting the Securities and current Coin of the United States;

To establish Post Offices and Post Roads;

To promote the Progress of Science and useful Arts, by securing for limited Times to Authors and Inventors the exclusive Right to their respective Writings and Discoveries;

To constitute Tribunals inferior to the supreme Court;

To define and punish Piracies and Felonies committed on the high Seas, and Offenses against the Law of Nations;

To declare War, grant Letters of Marque and Reprisal, and make Rules concerning Captures on Land and Water;

To raise and support Armies, but no Appropriation of Money to that Use shall be for a longer Term than two Years;

To provide and maintain a Navy;

The Constitution of the United States (cont.)

To make Rules for the Government and Regulation of the land and naval Forces;

To provide for calling forth the Militia to execute the Laws of the Union, suppress Insurrections, and repel Invasions;

To provide for organizing, arming, and disciplining the Militia, and for governing such Part of them as may be employed in the Service of the United States, reserving to the States respectively, the Appointment of the Officers, and the Authority of training the Militia according to the discipline prescribed by Congress;

To exercise exclusive Legislation in all Cases whatsoever, over such District (not exceeding ten Miles square) as may, by Cession of particular States, and the acceptance of Congress, become the Seat of the Government of the United States, and to exercise like Authority over all Places purchased by the Consent of the Legislature of the State in which the Same shall be, for the Erection of Forts, Magazines, Arsenals, dock-Yards, and other needful Buildings; And

To make all Laws which shall be necessary and proper for carrying into Execution the foregoing Powers, and all other Powers vested by this Constitution in the Government of the United States, or in any Department or Officer thereof.

Section 9 - Limits on Congress

[The Migration or Importation of such Persons as any of the States now existing shall think proper to admit, shall not be prohibited by the Congress prior to the Year one thousand eight hundred and eight, but a tax or duty may be imposed on such Importation, not exceeding ten dollars for each Person.] *Note: Amendment XIII nullified the words in brackets.*

The privilege of the Writ of Habeas Corpus shall not be suspended, unless when in Cases of Rebellion or Invasion the public Safety may require it.

No Bill of Attainder or ex post facto Law shall be passed. [No capitation, or other direct Tax shall be laid, unless in Proportion to the Census or Enumeration herein before directed to be taken.] *Note: Amendment XVI modified the sentence in brackets.*

No Tax or Duty shall be laid on Articles exported from any State.

No Preference shall be given by any Regulation of Commerce or Revenue to the Ports of one State over those of another: nor shall Vessels bound to, or from, one State, be obliged to enter, clear, or pay Duties in another.

No Money shall be drawn from the Treasury, but in Consequence of Appropriations made by Law; and a regular Statement and Account of the Receipts and Expenditures of all public Money shall be published from time to time.

The Constitution of the United States (cont.)

No Title of Nobility shall be granted by the United States: And no Person holding any Office of Profit or Trust under them, shall, without the Consent of the Congress, accept of any present, Emolument, Office, or Title, of any kind whatever, from any King, Prince, or foreign State.

Section 10 - Powers Prohibited of States
No State shall enter into any Treaty, Alliance, or Confederation; grant Letters of Marque and Reprisal; coin Money; emit Bills of Credit; make any Thing but gold and silver Coin a Tender in Payment of Debts; pass any Bill of Attainder, ex post facto Law, or Law impairing the Obligation of Contracts, or grant any Title of Nobility.

No State shall, without the Consent of the Congress, lay any Imposts or Duties on Imports or Exports, except what may be absolutely necessary for executing its inspection Laws: and the net Produce of all Duties and Imposts, laid by any State on Imports or Exports, shall be for the Use of the Treasury of the United States; and all such Laws shall be subject to the Revision and Controul of the Congress.

No State shall, without the Consent of Congress, lay any duty of Tonnage, keep Troops, or Ships of War in time of Peace, enter into any Agreement or Compact with another State, or with a foreign Power, or engage in War, unless actually invaded, or in such imminent Danger as will not admit of delay.

Article II. - The Executive Branch
Section 1 - The President
The exccutive Power shall be vested in a President of the United States of America. He shall hold his Office during the Term of four Years, and, together with the Vice President chosen for the same Term, be elected, as follows:

Each State shall appoint, in such Manner as the Legislature thereof may direct, a Number of Electors, equal to the whole Number of Senators and Representatives to which the State may be entitled in the Congress: but no Senator or Representative, or Person holding an Office of Trust or Profit under the United States, shall be appointed an Elector. [The Electors shall meet in their respective States, and vote by Ballot for two persons, of whom one at least shall not lie an Inhabitant of the same State with themselves. And they shall make a List of all the Persons voted for, and of the Number of Votes for each; which List they shall sign and certify, and transmit sealed to the Seat of the Government of the United States, directed to the President of the Senate. The President of the Senate shall, in the Presence of the Senate and House of Representatives, open all the Certificates, and the Votes shall then be counted. The Person having the greatest Number of Votes shall be the President, if such Number be a Majority of the whole Number of Electors appointed; and if there be more than one who have such Majority, and have an equal Number of Votes, then the House of Representatives shall immediately chuse by Ballot one of them for President; and if no Person have a Majority, then from the five highest on the List the said House shall in like Manner chuse the President. But in chusing the

The Constitution of the United States (cont.)

President, the Votes shall be taken by States, the Representation from each State having one Vote; a quorum for this Purpose shall consist of a Member or Members from two-thirds of the States, and a Majority of all the States shall be necessary to a Choice. In every Case, after the Choice of the President, the Person having the greatest Number of Votes of the Electors shall be the Vice President. But if there should remain two or more who have equal Votes, the Senate shall chuse from them by Ballot the Vice President.] *Note: Amendment XII changed the section in brackets.*

The Congress may determine the Time of chusing the Electors, and the Day on which they shall give their Votes; which Day shall be the same throughout the United States.

No person except a natural born Citizen, or a Citizen of the United States, at the time of the Adoption of this Constitution, shall be eligible to the Office of President; neither shall any Person be eligible to that Office who shall not have attained to the Age of thirty-five Years, and been fourteen Years a Resident within the United States. [In Case of the Removal of the President from Office, or of his Death, Resignation, or Inability to discharge the Powers and Duties of the said Office, the same shall devolve on the Vice President, and the Congress may by Law provide for the Case of Removal, Death, Resignation or Inability, both of the President and Vice President, declaring what Officer shall then act as President, and such Officer shall act accordingly, until the Disability be removed, or a President shall be elected.] *Note: Amendments XX and XXV changed the section in brackets.*

The President shall, at stated Times, receive for his Services, a Compensation, which shall neither be increased nor diminished during the Period for which he shall have been elected, and he shall not receive within that Period any other Emolument from the United States, or any of them.

Before he enter on the Execution of his Office, he shall take the following Oath or Affirmation:— "I do solemnly swear (or affirm) that I will faithfully execute the Office of President of the United States, and will to the best of my Ability, preserve, protect, and defend the Constitution of the United States."

Section 2 - Civilian Power Over Military, Cabinet, Pardon Power, Appointments
The President shall be Commander in Chief of the Army and Navy of the United States, and of the Militia of the several States, when called into the actual Service of the United States; he may require the Opinion, in writing, of the principal Officer in each of the executive Departments, upon any subject relating to the Duties of their respective Offices, and he shall have Power to Grant Reprieves and Pardons for Offenses against the United States, except in Cases of Impeachment.

He shall have Power, by and with the Advice and Consent of the Senate, to make Treaties, provided two-thirds of the Senators present concur; and he shall nominate, and by and with

The Constitution of the United States (cont.)

the Advice and Consent of the Senate, shall appoint Ambassadors, other public Ministers and Consuls, Judges of the supreme Court, and all other Officers of the United States, whose Appointments are not herein otherwise provided for, and which shall be established by Law: but the Congress may by Law vest the Appointment of such inferior Officers, as they think proper, in the President alone, in the Courts of Law, or in the Heads of Departments.

The President shall have Power to fill up all Vacancies that may happen during the Recess of the Senate, by granting Commissions which shall expire at the End of their next Session.

Section 3 - State of the Union, Convening Congress

He shall from time to time give to the Congress Information of the State of the Union, and recommend to their Consideration such Measures as he shall judge necessary and expedient; he may, on extraordinary Occasions, convene both Houses, or either of them, and in Case of Disagreement between them, with Respect to the Time of Adjournment, he may adjourn them to such Time as he shall think proper; he shall receive Ambassadors and other public Ministers; he shall take Care that the Laws be faithfully executed, and shall Commission all the Officers of the United States.

Section 4 - Disqualification

The President, Vice President and all civil Officers of the United States, shall be removed from Office on Impeachment for, and Conviction of, Treason, Bribery, or other high Crimes and Misdemeanors.

Article III. - The Judicial Branch
Section 1 - Judicial Powers

The judicial Power of the United States, shall be vested in one supreme Court, and in such inferior Courts as the Congress may from time to time ordain and establish. The Judges, both of the supreme and inferior Courts, shall hold their Offices during good Behavior, and shall, at stated Times, receive for their Services a Compensation which shall not be diminished during their Continuance in Office.

Section 2 - Trial by Jury, Original Jurisdiction, Jury Trials

The judicial Power shall extend to all Cases, in Law and Equity, arising under this Constitution, the Laws of the United States, and Treaties made, or which shall be made, under their Authority;—to all Cases affecting Ambassadors, other public Ministers and Consuls;—to all Cases of admiralty and maritime Jurisdiction;—to Controversies to which the United States shall be a Party;—to Controversies between two or more States;—[between a State and Citizens of another State;]—between Citizens of different States;—between Citizens of the same State claiming Lands under Grants of different States, and between a State, or the Citizens thereof, and foreign States, Citizens or Subjects. *Note: Amendment XI changed the words in brackets.*

The Constitution of the United States (cont.)

In all Cases affecting Ambassadors, other public Ministers and Consuls, and those in which a State shall be Party, the supreme Court shall have original Jurisdiction. In all the other Cases before mentioned, the supreme Court shall have appellate Jurisdiction, both as to Law and Fact, with such Exceptions, and under such Regulations as the Congress shall make.

The Trial of all Crimes, except in Cases of Impeachment, shall be by Jury; and such Trial shall be held in the State where the said Crimes shall have been committed; but when not committed within any State, the Trial shall be at such Place or Places as the Congress may by Law have directed.

Section 3 - Treason

Treason against the United States, shall consist only in levying War against them, or in adhering to their Enemies, giving them Aid and Comfort. No Person shall be convicted of Treason unless on the Testimony of two Witnesses to the same overt Act, or on Confession in open Court.

The Congress shall have power to declare the Punishment of Treason, but no Attainder of Treason shall work Corruption of Blood, or Forfeiture except during the Life of the Person attainted.

Article IV. - The States
Section 1 - Each State to Honor All Others

Full Faith and Credit shall be given in each State to the public Acts, Records, and judicial Proceedings of every other State. And the Congress may by general Laws prescribe the Manner in which such Acts, Records and Proceedings shall be proved, and the Effect thereof.

Section 2 - State Citizens, Extradition

The Citizens of each State shall be entitled to all Privileges and Immunities of Citizens in the several States.

A Person charged in any State with Treason, Felony, or other Crime, who shall flee from Justice, and be found in another State, shall on demand of the executive Authority of the State from which he fled, be delivered up, to be removed to the State having Jurisdiction of the Crime. [No Person held to Service or Labour in one State, under the Laws thereof, escaping into another, shall, in Consequence of any Law or Regulation therein, be discharged from such Service or Labour, But shall be delivered up on Claim of the Party to whom such Service or Labour may be due.] *Note: Amendment XIII changed the words in brackets.*

Section 3 - New States

New States may be admitted by the Congress into this Union; but no new States shall be formed or erected within the Jurisdiction of any other State; nor any State be formed by the Junction of two or more States, or parts of States, without the Consent of the Legislatures of the States concerned as well as of the Congress.

The Constitution of the United States (cont.)

The Congress shall have Power to dispose of and make all needful Rules and Regulations respecting the Territory or other Property belonging to the United States; and nothing in this Constitution shall be so construed as to Prejudice any Claims of the United States, or of any particular State.

Section 4 - Republican Government

The United States shall guarantee to every State in this Union a Republican Form of Government, and shall protect each of them against Invasion; and on Application of the Legislature, or of the Executive (when the Legislature cannot be convened) against domestic Violence.

Article V. - Amendment

The Congress, whenever two-thirds of both Houses shall deem it necessary, shall propose Amendments to this Constitution, or, on the Application of the Legislatures of two-thirds of the several States, shall call a Convention for proposing Amendments, which, in either Case, shall be valid to all Intents and Purposes, as part of this Constitution, when ratified by the Legislatures of three-fourths of the several States, or by Conventions in three-fourths thereof, as the one or the other Mode of Ratification may be proposed by the Congress; Provided [that no Amendment which may be made prior to the Year One thousand eight hundred and eight shall in any Manner affect the first and fourth Clauses in the Ninth Section of the first Article; and] that no State, without its Consent, shall be deprived of its equal Suffrage in the Senate. *Note: Amendment XIII nullified the words in brackets.*

Article VI. - The United States

All Debts contracted and Engagements entered into, before the Adoption of this Constitution, shall be as valid against the United States under this Constitution, as under the Confederation.

This Constitution, and the Laws of the United States which shall be made in Pursuance thereof; and all Treaties made, or which shall be made, under the Authority of the United States, shall be the supreme Law of the Land; and the Judges in every State shall be bound thereby, any Thing in the Constitution or Laws of any State to the Contrary notwithstanding.

The Senators and Representatives before mentioned, and the Members of the several State Legislatures, and all executive and judicial Officers, both of the United States and of the several States, shall be bound by Oath or Affirmation, to support this Constitution; but no religious Test shall ever be required as a Qualification to any Office or public Trust under the United States.

Article VII. - Ratification Documents

The Ratification of the Conventions of nine States, shall be sufficient for the Establishment of this Constitution between the States so ratifying the Same.

The Constitution of the United States (cont.)

Done in Convention by the Unanimous Consent of the States present the Seventeenth Day of September in the Year of our Lord one thousand seven hundred and Eighty-seven and of the Independence of the United States of America the Twelfth. In Witness whereof We have hereunto subscribed our Names.

George Washington - President and deputy from Virginia
New Hampshire - John Langdon, Nicholas Gilman
Massachusetts - Nathaniel Gorham, Rufus King
Connecticut - Wm. Saml. Johnson, Roger Sherman
New York - Alexander Hamilton
New Jersey - Wil Livingston, David Brearley, Wm. Paterson, Jona. Dayton
Pennsylvania - B. Franklin, Thomas Mifflin, Robt Morris, Geo. Clymer, Thos FitzSimons, Jared Ingersoll, James Wilson, Gouv Morris
Delaware - Geo. Read, Gunning Bedford jun, John Dickinson, Richard Bassett, Jaco. Broom
Maryland - James McHenry, Dan of St Thos. Jenifer, Danl Carroll
Virginia - John Blair, James Madison Jr.
North Carolina - Wm. Blount, Richd. Dobbs Spaight, Hu Williamson
South Carolina - J. Rutledge, Charles Cotesworth Pinckney, Charles Pinckney, Pierce Butler
Georgia - William Few, Abr Baldwin
Attest: William Jackson, Secretary

Amendment I - Freedom of Religion, Press, Expression (Ratified 12/15/1791)
Congress shall make no law respecting an establishment of religion, or prohibiting the free exercise thereof; or abridging the freedom of speech, or of the press; or the right of the people peaceably to assemble, and to petition the Government for a redress of grievances.

Amendment II - Right to Bear Arms (Ratified 12/15/1791)
A well-regulated Militia, being necessary to the security of a free State, the right of the people to keep and bear Arms, shall not be infringed.

Amendment III - Quartering of Soldiers (Ratified 12/15/1791)
No Soldier shall, in time of peace be quartered in any house, without the consent of the Owner, nor in time of war, but in a manner to be prescribed by law.

Amendment IV - Search and Seizure (Ratified 12/15/1791)
The right of the people to be secure in their persons, houses, papers, and effects, against unreasonable searches and seizures, shall not be violated, and no Warrants shall issue, but upon probable cause, supported by Oath or affirmation, and particularly describing the place to be searched, and the persons or things to be seized.

The Constitution of the United States (cont.)

Amendment V - Trial and Punishment, Compensation for Takings (Ratified 12/15/1791)

No person shall be held to answer for a capital, or otherwise infamous crime, unless on a presentment or indictment of a Grand Jury, except in cases arising in the land or naval forces, or in the Militia, when in actual service in time of War or public danger; nor shall any person be subject for the same offense to be twice put in jeopardy of life or limb; nor shall be compelled in any criminal case to be a witness against himself, nor be deprived of life, liberty, or property, without due process of law; nor shall private property be taken for public use, without just compensation.

Amendment VI - Right to Speedy Trial, Confrontation of Witnesses (Ratified 12/15/1791)

In all criminal prosecutions, the accused shall enjoy the right to a speedy and public trial, by an impartial jury of the State and district wherein the crime shall have been committed, which district shall have been previously ascertained by law, and to be informed of the nature and cause of the accusation; to be confronted with the witnesses against him; to have compulsory process for obtaining witnesses in his favor, and to have the Assistance of Counsel for his defence.

Amendment VII - Trial by Jury in Civil Cases (Ratified 12/15/1791)

In Suits at common law, where the value in controversy shall exceed twenty dollars, the right of trial by jury shall be preserved, and no fact tried by a jury, shall be otherwise reexamined in any Court of the United States, than according to the rules of the common law.

Amendment VIII - Cruel and Unusual Punishment (Ratified 12/15/1791)

Excessive bail shall not be required, nor excessive fines imposed, nor cruel and unusual punishments inflicted.

Amendment IX - Construction of Constitution (Ratified 12/15/1791)

The enumeration in the Constitution, of certain rights, shall not be construed to deny or disparage others retained by the people.

Amendment X - Powers of the States and People (Ratified 12/15/1791)

The powers not delegated to the United States by the Constitution, nor prohibited by it to the States, are reserved to the States respectively, or to the people.

Amendment XI - Judicial Limits (Ratified 2/7/1795)

The Judicial power of the United States shall not be construed to extend to any suit in law or equity, commenced or prosecuted against one of the United States by Citizens of another State, or by Citizens or Subjects of any Foreign State.

The Constitution of the United States (cont.)

Amendment XII - Choosing the President, Vice President (Ratified 6/15/1804)

The Electors shall meet in their respective states, and vote by ballot for President and Vice President, one of whom, at least, shall not be an inhabitant of the same state with themselves; they shall name in their ballots the person voted for as President, and in distinct ballots the person voted for as Vice President, and they shall make distinct lists of all persons voted for as President, and of all persons voted for as Vice President and of the number of votes for each, which lists they shall sign and certify, and transmit sealed to the seat of the government of the United States, directed to the President of the Senate;

The President of the Senate shall, in the presence of the Senate and House of Representatives, open all the certificates and the votes shall then be counted;—The person having the greatest Number of votes for President, shall be the President, if such number be a majority of the whole number of Electors appointed; and if no person have such majority, then from the persons having the highest numbers not exceeding three on the list of those voted for as President, the House of Representatives shall choose immediately, by ballot, the President. But in choosing the President, the votes shall be taken by states, the representation from each state having one vote; a quorum for this purpose shall consist of a member or members from two-thirds of the states, and a majority of all the states shall be necessary to a choice. [And if the House of Representatives shall not choose a President whenever the right of choice shall devolve upon them, before the fourth day of March next following, then the Vice President shall act as President, as in the case of the death or other constitutional disability of the President.] *Note: Amendment XX changed the words in brackets.*

The person having the greatest number of votes as Vice President, shall be the Vice President, if such number be a majority of the whole number of Electors appointed, and if no person have a majority, then from the two highest numbers on the list, the Senate shall choose the Vice President; a quorum for the purpose shall consist of two-thirds of the whole number of Senators, and a majority of the whole number shall be necessary to a choice. But no person constitutionally ineligible to the office of President shall be eligible to that of Vice President of the United States.

Amendment XIII - Slavery Abolished (Ratified 12/6/1865)

Section 1. Neither slavery nor involuntary servitude, except as a punishment for crime whereof the party shall have been duly convicted, shall exist within the United States, or any place subject to their jurisdiction.

Section 2. Congress shall have power to enforce this article by appropriate legislation.

The Constitution of the United States (cont.)

Amendment XIV - Citizenship Rights (Ratified 7/9/1868)

Section 1. All persons born or naturalized in the United States, and subject to the jurisdiction thereof, are citizens of the United States and of the State wherein they reside. No State shall make or enforce any law which shall abridge the privileges or immunities of citizens of the United States; nor shall any State deprive any person of life, liberty, or property, without due process of law; nor deny to any person within its jurisdiction the equal protection of the laws.

Section 2. Representatives shall be apportioned among the several States according to their respective numbers, counting the whole number of persons in each State, excluding Indians not taxed. But when the right to vote at any election for the choice of electors for President and Vice President of the United States, Representatives in Congress, the Executive and Judicial officers of a State, or the members of the Legislature thereof, is denied to any of the male inhabitants of such State, being twenty-one years of age, and citizens of the United States, or in any way abridged, except for participation in rebellion, or other crime, the basis of representation therein shall be reduced in the proportion which the number of such male citizens shall bear to the whole number of male citizens twenty-one years of age in such State.

Section 3. [No person shall be a Senator or Representative in Congress, or elector of President and Vice President, or hold any office, civil or military, under the United States, or under any State, who, having previously taken an oath, as a member of Congress, or as an officer of the United States, or as a member of any State legislature, or as an executive or judicial officer of any State, to support the Constitution of the United States, shall have engaged in insurrection or rebellion against the same, or given aid or comfort to the enemies thereof. But Congress may by a vote of two-thirds of each House, remove such disability.] *Note: This clause was deleted by Congress in 1898.*

Section 4. The validity of the public debt of the United States, authorized by law, including debts incurred for payment of pensions and bounties for services in suppressing insurrection or rebellion, shall not be questioned. But neither the United States nor any State shall assume or pay any debt or obligation incurred in aid of insurrection or rebellion against the United States, or any claim for the loss or emancipation of any slave; but all such debts, obligations, and claims shall be held illegal and void.

Section 5. The Congress shall have power to enforce, by appropriate legislation, the provisions of this article.

Amendment XV - Race No Bar to Vote (Ratified 2/3/1870)

Section 1. The right of citizens of the United States to vote shall not be denied or abridged by the United States or by any State on account of race, color, or previous condition of servitude.

Section 2. The Congress shall have power to enforce this article by appropriate legislation.

The Constitution of the United States (cont.)

Amendment XVI - Income Taxes Authorized (Ratified 2/3/1913)

The Congress shall have power to lay and collect taxes on incomes, from whatever source derived, without apportionment among the several States, and without regard to any census or enumeration.

Amendment XVII - Senators Elected by Popular Vote (Ratified 4/8/1913)

The Senate of the United States shall be composed of two Senators from each State, elected by the people thereof, for six years; and each Senator shall have one vote. The electors in each State shall have the qualifications requisite for electors of the most numerous branch of the State legislatures.

When vacancies happen in the representation of any State in the Senate, the executive authority of such State shall issue writs of election to fill such vacancies: Provided, that the legislature of any State may empower the executive thereof to make temporary appointments until the people fill the vacancies by election as the legislature may direct.

This amendment shall not be so construed as to affect the election or term of any Senator chosen before it becomes valid as part of the Constitution.

Amendment XVIII - Liquor Abolished (Ratified 1/16/1919)

Section 1. After one year from the ratification of this article the manufacture, sale, or transportation of intoxicating liquors within, the importation thereof into, or the exportation thereof from the United States and all territory subject to the jurisdiction thereof for beverage purposes is hereby prohibited.

Section 2. The Congress and the several States shall have concurrent power to enforce this article by appropriate legislation.

Section 3. This article shall be inoperative unless it shall have been ratified as an amendment to the Constitution by the legislatures of the several States, as provided in the Constitution, within seven years from the date of the submission hereof to the States by the Congress.
Note: Amendment XVIII was repealed by Amendment XXI.

Amendment XIX - Women's Suffrage (Ratified 8/18/1920)

The right of citizens of the United States to vote shall not be denied or abridged by the United States or by any State on account of sex. Congress shall have power to enforce this article by appropriate legislation.

The Constitution of
the United States (cont.)

Amendment XX - Presidential, Congressional Terms (Ratified 1/23/1933)

Section 1. The terms of the President and Vice President shall end at noon on the 20th day of January, and the terms of Senators and Representatives at noon on the 3d day of January, of the years in which such terms would have ended if this article had not been ratified; and the terms of their successors shall then begin.

Section 2. The Congress shall assemble at least once in every year, and such meeting shall begin at noon on the 3d day of January, unless they shall by law appoint a different day.

Section 3. If, at the time fixed for the beginning of the term of the President, the President elect shall have died, the Vice President elect shall become President. If a President shall not have been chosen before the time fixed for the beginning of his term, or if the President elect shall have failed to qualify, then the Vice President elect shall act as President until a President shall have qualified; and the Congress may by law provide for the case wherein neither a President elect nor a Vice President elect shall have qualified, declaring who shall then act as President, or the manner in which one who is to act shall be selected, and such person shall act accordingly until a President or Vice President shall have qualified.

Section 4. The Congress may by law provide for the case of the death of any of the persons from whom the House of Representatives may choose a President whenever the right of choice shall have devolved upon them, and for the case of the death of any of the persons from whom the Senate may choose a Vice President whenever the right of choice shall have devolved upon them.

Section 5. Sections 1 and 2 shall take effect on the 15th day of October following the ratification of this article.

Section 6. This article shall be inoperative unless it shall have been ratified as an amendment to the Constitution by the legislatures of three-fourths of the several States within seven years from the date of its submission.

Amendment XXI - Amendment XVIII Repealed (Ratified 12/5/1933)

Section 1. The eighteenth article of amendment to the Constitution of the United States is hereby repealed.

Section 2. The transportation or importation into any State, Territory, or possession of the United States for delivery or use therein of intoxicating liquors, in violation of the laws thereof, is hereby prohibited.

Section 3. This article shall be inoperative unless it shall have been ratified as an amendment to the Constitution by conventions in the several States, as provided in the Constitution, within seven years from the date of the submission hereof to the States by the Congress.

The Constitution of the United States (cont.)

Amendment XXII - Presidential Term Limits (Ratified 2/27/1951)

Section 1. No person shall be elected to the office of the President more than twice, and no person who has held the office of President, or acted as President, for more than two years of a term to which some other person was elected President shall be elected to the office of the President more than once. But this Article shall not apply to any person holding the office of President, when this Article was proposed by the Congress, and shall not prevent any person who may be holding the office of President, or acting as President, during the term within which this Article becomes operative from holding the office of President or acting as President during the remainder of such term.

Section 2. This article shall be inoperative unless it shall have been ratified as an amendment to the Constitution by the legislatures of three-fourths of the several States within seven years from the date of its submission to the States by the Congress.

Amendment XXIII - Presidential Vote for District of Columbia (Ratified 3/29/1961)

Section 1. The District constituting the seat of Government of the United States shall appoint in such manner as the Congress may direct: A number of electors of President and Vice President equal to the whole number of Senators and Representatives in Congress to which the District would be entitled if it were a State, but in no event more than the least populous State; they shall be in addition to those appointed by the States, but they shall be considered, for the purposes of the election of President and Vice President, to be electors appointed by a State; and they shall meet in the District and perform such duties as provided by the twelfth article of amendment.

Section 2. The Congress shall have power to enforce this article by appropriate legislation.

Amendment XXIV - Poll Tax Barred (Ratified 1/23/1964)

Section 1. The right of citizens of the United States to vote in any primary or other election for President or Vice President, for electors for President or Vice President, or for Senator or Representative in Congress, shall not be denied or abridged by the United States or any State by reason of failure to pay any poll tax or other tax.

Section 2. The Congress shall have power to enforce this article by appropriate legislation.

Amendment XXV - Presidential Disability and Succession (Ratified 2/10/1967)

Section 1. In case of the removal of the President from office or of his death or resignation, the Vice President shall become President.

Section 2. Whenever there is a vacancy in the office of the Vice President, the President shall nominate a Vice President who shall take office upon confirmation by a majority vote of both Houses of Congress.

The Constitution of the United States (cont.)

Section 3. Whenever the President transmits to the President pro tempore of the Senate and the Speaker of the House of Representatives his written declaration that he is unable to discharge the powers and duties of his office, and until he transmits to them a written declaration to the contrary, such powers and duties shall be discharged by the Vice President as Acting President.

Section 4. Whenever the Vice President and a majority of either the principal officers of the executive departments or of such other body as Congress may by law provide, transmit to the President pro tempore of the Senate and the Speaker of the House of Representatives their written declaration that the President is unable to discharge the powers and duties of his office, the Vice President shall immediately assume the powers and duties of the office as Acting President.

Thereafter, when the President transmits to the President pro tempore of the Senate and the Speaker of the House of Representatives his written declaration that no inability exists, he shall resume the powers and duties of his office unless the Vice President and a majority of either the principal officers of the executive department or of such other body as Congress may by law provide, transmit within four days to the President pro tempore of the Senate and the Speaker of the House of Representatives their written declaration that the President is unable to discharge the powers and duties of his office. Thereupon Congress shall decide the issue, assembling within forty-eight hours for that purpose if not in session. If the Congress, within twenty-one days after receipt of the latter written declaration, or, if Congress is not in session, within twenty-one days after Congress is required to assemble, determines by two-thirds vote of both Houses that the President is unable to discharge the powers and duties of his office, the Vice President shall continue to discharge the same as Acting President; otherwise, the President shall resume the powers and duties of his office.

Amendment XXVI - Voting Age Set to 18 Years (Ratified 7/1/1971)
Section 1. The right of citizens of the United States, who are eighteen years of age or older, to vote, shall not be denied or abridged by the United States or by any State on account of age.

Section 2. The Congress shall have power to enforce this article by appropriate legislation.

Amendment XXVII - Congressional Pay Increases (Ratified 5/7/1992)
No law, varying the compensation for the services of the Senators and Representatives, shall take effect until an election of Representatives shall have intervened.

The U.S. Constitution Warm-ups
The Preamble

Name/Date _____

The Preamble 1

Write a short definition for each word. Use a dictionary if you need help.

preamble: _____

domestic: _____

tranquility: _____

posterity: _____

ordain: _____

Name/Date _____

The Preamble 2

According to the Preamble, what are three reasons for writing the Constitution?

_____

_____

_____

_____

_____

Name/Date _____

The Preamble 3

Spelling and capitalization rules were not uniform at the time the founding fathers wrote the Constitution.

What word is spelled incorrectly in the Preamble? _____

Why do you think words like Welfare, Blessings, and Liberty are capitalized?

_____

Name/Date _____

The Preamble 4

Memorize the Preamble. Recite the Preamble as though you were one of the Founding Fathers. Be dramatic and convincing.

Name/Date _____

The Preamble 5

If you could rewrite the Preamble to the Constitution, what changes would you make? Include at least three changes and the reasons you would make them. Write your answer on another sheet of paper.

The U.S. Constitution Warm-ups
Article 1: The Legislative Branch

Name/Date _____

Congress 1 (Art. 1: Sect. 1-2)

Write a short definition for each word. Feel free to use a dictionary.

legislative: _____

requisite: _____

enumeration: _____

subsequent: _____

Name/Date _____

Congress 2 (Art. 1: Sect. 1-2)

List the three qualifications for members of the House of Representatives.

_____

_____

_____

_____

Name/Date _____

Congress 3 (Art. 1: Sect. 1-2)

The number of members in the House of Representatives from each state is based on population. The Constitution requires a new census every 10 years. Do you think that is too often, not often enough, or about right? Explain your answer on another sheet of paper.

Name/Date _____

Congress 4 (Art. 1: Sect. 1-2)

1. How long is the term for a member of the House of Representatives? _____
2. What is the leader of the House of Representatives called? _____
   _____
3. Who elects the leader of the House of Representatives? _____

Name/Date _____

Congress 5

Would you like to be elected as a member of the House of Representatives? Why or why not?

_____

_____

_____

_____

The U.S. Constitution Warm-ups
Article 1: The Legislative Branch

Name/Date _____

Congress 6
(Art. 1: Sect. 1-3)

1. What two groups make up the U.S. Congress?

   _____

   _____

   _____

2. How many senators does each state have?

   _____

3. What is the length of the term of office for a senator?

   _____

4. Who is the leader of the Senate?

   _____

Name/Date _____

Congress 7 (Art. 1: Sect. 3)

Write a short definition for each word on your own paper. Feel free to use a dictionary.

pro tempore   concurrence
impeachment   liable
affirmation

Name/Date _____

Congress 8 (Art. 1: Sect. 3)

List the three qualifications for senators:

_____

_____

_____

Name/Date _____

Congress 9 (Art. 1: Sect. 1-3)

Representatives of small states with low populations worried that the larger states would control the government if the number of representatives to Congress was based on population. On another sheet of paper, explain how the Constitution addressed this issue.

Name/Date _____

Congress 10 (Art. 1: Sect. 1-3)

On another sheet of paper, create a table comparing qualifications and terms of office of members of the House of Representatives and members of the Senate.

The U.S. Constitution Warm-ups
Article 1: The Legislative Branch

Name/Date _____

Congress 11

1. How many members of the House of Representatives does your state have in Congress? _____

2. Name the two senators from your state.

_____

_____

3. Who is currently the Speaker of the House? _____

Name/Date _____

Congress 12

Imagine being elected as a senator from your state. On your first day, you are invited to give a short speech to introduce yourself, explain why you will make a good senator, and what you hope to accomplish as a member of Congress. Give your speech to the class.

Name/Date _____

Congress 13 (Art. 1: Sect. 4–10)

Write a short definition for each word. Use a dictionary if you need help.

adjourn: _____

quorum: _____

revenue: _____

veto: _____

Name/Date _____

Congress 14 (Art. 1: Sect. 5)

U.S. citizens have the right to elect members of Congress by secret ballot. However, voting by members of Congress while in session is a matter of public record. Do you think that is fair? Explain why or why not on another sheet of paper.

Name/Date _____

Congress 15 (Art. 1: Sect. 7)

What is the difference between a bill and a law?

_____

_____

_____

_____

The U.S. Constitution Warm-ups
Article 1: The Legislative Branch

Name/Date _____

Congress 16 (Art. 1: Sect. 7)

On another sheet of paper or poster board, create a flow chart showing how bills become laws. Include what happens if the bill does or does not pass in both houses, if the president does or does not sign the bill, and if the president does not sign the bill and Congress adjourns during the next 10 days.

Name/Date _____

Congress 17

If you could introduce a bill in Congress to change a current law or create a new law, what would it be? On your own paper, write a summary of your bill.

NEW LAW

Name/Date _____

Congress 18 (Art. 1: Sect. 8)

The Constitution gave Congress many powers. List five powers it has.

_____

_____

_____

_____

_____

_____

Name/Date _____

Congress 19 (Art. 1: Sect. 9)

The Constitution placed limits on the powers of Congress. List three limits on Congress.

_____

_____

_____

_____

_____

Name/Date _____

Congress 20 (Art. 1: Sect. 10)

Select one of the limits imposed on the states by the Constitution in Article 1: Section 10. List several pros and cons for the limit.

Pros

_____

_____

_____

_____

Cons

_____

_____

_____

_____

The U.S. Constitution Warm-ups
Article 2: The Executive Branch

Name/Date _____

The President 1 (Art. 2)

Write a short definition for each word on your own paper. Use a dictionary if you need help.

executive   reprieve

emolument   militia

Name/Date _____

The President 2 (Art. 2: Sect. 1)

1. T   F   The President of the United States is elected for a four-year term.
2. T   F   The vice president is commander in chief of the Army and Navy.
3. T   F   The president must be at least 50 years old.
4. T   F   Members of Congress elect the president and vice president.

Name/Date _____

The President 3 (Art. 2: Sect. 1)

Use reference sources to learn more about the Electoral College. On another sheet of paper, explain the difference between election by popular vote and the method used to elect the president and vice president.

Name/Date _____

The President 4 (Art. 2: Sect. 1)

At the time the Constitution was written, the majority of people could not read or write. There were few newspapers, no radio, television, or computers. Because circumstances have changed, some people believe the Electoral College should be eliminated and that the president and vice president should be elected by popular vote. Debate this issue with a classmate.

Name/Date _____

The President 5 (Art. 2: Sect. 1)

1. How many electoral votes does your state have?

    _____

2. List the number of electoral votes for each of these states.

    _____ New York

    _____ California

    _____ New Mexico

    _____ Alaska

    _____ New Jersey

    _____ Alabama

    _____ Pennsylvania

    _____ Michigan

The U.S. Constitution Warm-ups
Article 2: The Executive Branch

Name/Date _____

The President 6 (Art. 2: Sect. 1-3)

1. List the three qualifications someone must meet to be president.

   _____

   _____

2. List three duties of the president that are specified in the Constitution. _____

   _____

   _____

Name/Date _____

The President 7 (Art. 2: Sect. 1)

Originally the president was the person with the most electoral votes, and the vice president was the person with the second most votes. This was later changed by the Twelfth Amendment.

On another sheet of paper, write what you think would happen if the president and vice president were chosen this way today.

Name/Date _____

The President 8

Answer these questions on your own paper.

1. Who is the current president?

2. Who is the current vice president?

3. The Constitution requires that the president be a natural-born citizen of the United States. Do you think that requirement should be changed? Why or why not?

Name/Date _____

The President 9

If you could put a limit on power or add a duty for the president, what would it be? Why?

_____

_____

_____

_____

_____

Name/Date _____

The President 10 (Art. 2: Sect. 1)

Congress cannot raise or lower the president's salary during the term of office. If that were not specified in the Constitution, what do you think might happen if a president were very popular or unpopular with Congress?

_____

_____

_____

_____

The U.S. Constitution Warm-ups
Article 2: The Executive Branch

Name/Date _____

The President 11 (Art. 2: Sect. 4)

Answer the following questions on your own paper.

1. Under what circumstances can the president, vice president, and other civil officers be removed from office?

2. Do you think this is fair? Why or why not?

Name/Date _____

The President 12 (Art. 2)

In your opinion, what is the most important duty of the president? Explain your answer on another sheet of paper.

Name/Date _____

The President 13 (Art. 2: Sect. 4)

The president selects people to be his advisors. Those who are directly responsible to him are called Cabinet members. They head various important government departments. Learn more about one Cabinet position. Answer the questions.

1. Which Cabinet position did you choose? _____
2. When was it established? _____
3. Who currently holds this position? _____
4. What are five areas of responsibility for this position? _____
_____

Name/Date _____

The President 14

On another sheet of paper, write a letter to one of these people expressing your view on a current issue: the president, a member of Congress, your state governor, or any member of the president's Cabinet.

Name/Date _____

The President 15

The form of government established by the Constitution is a republican form, rather than a democracy. In a true democracy, the people would directly elect all officials and vote directly on whether to pass laws. Which form do you think would be better (and more workable)? Give three or more reasons for your answer. Answer on your own paper.

The U.S. Constitution Warm-ups
Article 3: The Judicial Branch

Name/Date _____

The Judicial Branch 1 (Art. 3)

Write a short definition for each word. Use a dictionary if you need help.

judicial: _____

inferior: _____

jurisdiction: _____

appellate: _____

Name/Date _____

The Judicial Branch 2 (Art. 3)

1. The Supreme Court hears all cases affecting _____ and other public ministers and consuls.
2. A trial of all crimes shall be trial by jury except in the case of _____.
3. Congress cannot _____ the salary of Supreme Court judges while they hold office.
4. _____ has the power to declare the punishment for treason.

Name/Date _____

The Judicial Branch 3 (Art. 3)

Use reference sources to learn more about the judicial system. In your own words, describe what "trial by jury" means.

_____

_____

_____

_____

_____

Name/Date _____

The Judicial Branch 4 (Art. 3)

Why is trial by jury an important right of citizens of the United States?

_____

_____

_____

_____

_____

Name/Date _____

The Judicial Branch 5 (Art. 3)

In the United States, people who fill most important government positions are elected for a specific length of time. The president appoints justices of the Supreme Court who have no term limit. List several pros and cons for this.

Pros

_____

_____

_____

Cons

_____

_____

_____

The U.S. Constitution Warm-ups
Articles 4, 5, and 6

Name/Date _____

_____

The States 1
(Art. 4: Sect. 3)

1. T F New states can join the United States with approval by Congress.

2. T F Congress can decide to divide a large state into two or more smaller ones without the approval of the states themselves.

3. T F Two states can join together to create a new state only with approval by Congress.

4. T F The Constitution grants a republican form of government to each state.

5. T F If one state declares war on another state, the federal government cannot get involved.

Missibama

Name/Date _____

The States 2 (Art. 4: Sect. 2)

What happens if a person who commits a crime in one state goes to another state?

_____

_____

_____

Name/Date _____

Amending the Constitution 1 (Art. 5)

1. What fraction of Congress must agree to a proposal for an amendment to the Constitution? _____

2. What does ratified mean? _____

3. How many states must approve an amendment before it becomes part of the Constitution? _____

Name/Date _____

Amending the Constitution 2 (Art. 5)

If you could propose an amendment to the Constitution, what would it be? Describe your amendment and reasons on another sheet of paper.

AMENDMENT XXVIII

Name/Date _____

Upholding the Constitution (Art. 6)

According to Article 6, who is required to promise to uphold the Constitution?

_____

_____

_____

_____

The U.S. Constitution Warm-ups
Review Articles 1 through 7

Name/Date _____

Review 1

List the term of office for each person as specified in the Constitution.

1. President _____   2. Vice President
                            _____

3. Senator _____   4. Representative
                            _____

5. Cabinet   6. Supreme Court
   member _____   judge _____

Name/Date _____

Review 2

Write "L" for Legislative, "E" for Executive, or "J" for Judicial for each position.

1. ___ President
2. ___ Cabinet member
3. ___ Federal court judge
4. ___ Senator
5. ___ Justice of the Supreme Court
6. ___ Speaker of the House

Name/Date _____

Review 3

What is the minimum age specified in the Constitution for each position?

1. _____ Senator
2. _____ President
3. _____ Vice President
4. _____ Supreme Court judge
5. _____ Cabinet member
6. _____ Representative

Name/Date _____

Review 4

1. How many of the state conventions needed to ratify the Constitution before it became a binding legal document?

   _____

2. When did the Constitution become a binding legal document?

   _____

Name/Date _____

Review 5

Article VI lists those who must promise to uphold the Constitution. Write "yes" or "no" for each group to indicate whether or not they must make that promise.

1. _____ the president   2. _____ all eligible voters
3. _____ all judges   4. _____ all members of the military
5. _____ all members of Congress   6. _____ everyone over 21
7. _____ all state governors   8. _____ all Cabinet members
9. _____ all children of the president   10. _____ the president's spouse

---

 # The U.S. Constitution Warm-ups
Extension Activities

Name/Date _____

Extension Activity 1

Prepare a two-minute speech for or against ratifying the Constitution from the point of view of one of these people: a slave in Georgia; a wealthy, educated woman in Boston; a former British soldier; the governor of one of the 13 colonies; a religious leader, such as a priest, rabbi, or minister; a merchant in New York City; a farmer in Maine. Include reasons and examples for your opinion. Present your speech to the class.

Name/Date _____

Extension Activity 2

Complete one of the following:
• Prepare a poster showing the three branches of the government and the checks and balances each have on the other.
• Write a biography of one of the people who signed the Constitution.
• Write a report about the Constitutional Convention.
• Write a poem or song or perform a short puppet show about any aspect of the Constitution.

Name/Date _____

Extension Activity 3

Write a one-minute radio ad or design a poster to convince others to ratify the Bill of Rights. Present your ad to the class.

Name/Date _____

Extension Activity 4

Imagine being a member of the Constitution publicity department. It's your job to design a T-shirt to promote ratifying the Constitution. Show your design on another sheet of paper. Feel free to use computer clip art in your design.

Name/Date _____

_____

Extension Activity 5

Use a search engine to find five websites about the Constitution. Write the addresses of the sites.

_____
_____
_____
_____
_____
_____
_____
_____
_____
_____
_____
_____

Circle the address of the site you liked best. On another sheet of paper, write a short review telling others why you liked it and why it would be useful to other students.

The U.S. Constitution Warm-ups
The Bill of Rights: Amendments I through X

Name/Date _____

Bill of Rights 1 (Amend. I)

List five "rights" granted to citizens of the United States by Amendment I.

_____

_____

_____

_____

_____

Name/Date _____

Bill of Rights 2 (Amend. I)

Amendment I allows freedom of speech. Do you think everyone should have the right to say anything about anyone or anything without restriction? Why or why not?

_____

_____

_____

_____

Name/Date _____

Bill of Rights 3 (Amend. I-X)

Write a short definition for each word. Feel free to use a dictionary.

abridge: _____

quartered: _____

seizure: _____

indictment: _____

Name/Date _____

Bill of Rights 4 (Amend. I)

Amendment I guarantees freedom of religion. What restrictions, if any, do you think should be placed on this right? If none, explain why.

_____

_____

_____

_____

Name/Date _____

Bill of Rights 5 (Amend. II-V)

Write the number of the Amendment (2 through 5) for each item.

1. _____ Freedom from unreasonable searches
2. _____ The right to bear arms
3. _____ The right not to testify against yourself in a court
4. _____ The right not to have soldiers quartered in your home during peacetime
5. _____ The right not to be tried twice for the same crime

The U.S. Constitution Warm-ups
The Bill of Rights: Amendments I through X

Name/Date _____

Bill of Rights 6 (Amend. II)

Amendment II gives citizens the right to keep and bear arms.

1. What are "arms"? _____

_____

2. Some people believe our society would be safer if private citizens could not own weapons. Debate this issue with a classmate.

Name/Date _____

Bill of Rights 7 (Amend. III)

Amendment III gives Congress the right to have people provide room and board for soldiers during time of war. How would you feel if your family were required to provide food, housing, etc., for five soldiers? How would that affect you personally? Write your answer on another sheet of paper.

Name/Date _____

Bill of Rights 8 (Amend. IV)

1. What does seized mean? _____

_____

2. According to Amendment IV, what provisions must be met before a person or their property can be searched or seized?

_____

_____

Name/Date _____

Bill of Rights 9 (Amend. I-V)

Answer these questions on your own paper.

1. What right do people exercise if they "plead the fifth amendment"?

2. Of all the rights granted in the first five amendments, which do you think is the most important? Why?

Name/Date _____

Bill of Rights 10 (Amend. V)

Amendment V allows the government to take private property for public use, but it must pay the property owner a fair price. How would you feel about this if you found out the government wanted to tear down your home so they could build a road or public park there?

_____

_____

_____

_____

The U.S. Constitution Warm-ups
The Bill of Rights: Amendments I through X

Name/Date _____

_____

Bill of Rights 11 (Amend. VI)

Write "Y" for yes if Amendment VI grants the right. Write "N" for no if it does not.

1. _____ The right to call witnesses, even if they don't want to testify

2. _____ The right to have 13 people on the jury

3. _____ The right to have any judge they want

4. _____ The right to a speedy, public trial

5. _____ The right to confront witnesses against them

6. _____ The right to pay a fine instead of going to court

Name/Date _____

Bill of Rights 12 (Amend. VI, VII, and VIII)

Write the number of the Amendment (6 through 8) for each item.

1. _____ The right to a speedy trial
2. _____ The right to have a reasonable amount set as bail
3. _____ The right to a public trial
4. _____ The right to have a lawyer
5. _____ The right not to be subjected to cruel and unusual punishment

Name/Date _____

Bill of Rights 13 (Amend. IX)

Amendment IX states that in addition to the rights listed in the first eight amendments, citizens have other rights not listed. On your own paper, list some of the other rights we take for granted that are not listed in the first eight amendments.

Name/Date _____

Bill of Rights 14 (Amend. X)

In your own words, explain what the tenth amendment means.

_____

_____

_____

_____

Name/Date _____

Bill of Rights 15 (Amend. I-X)

On another sheet of paper, create your own "Bill of Rights." List ten rights to which you are entitled as a member of a family, school, city, country, etc. Do not include any listed in the first ten amendments to the Constitution.

The U.S. Constitution Warm-ups
Amendments XI and XII

Name/Date _____

Amendments XI and XII

Write a short definition for each word. Use a dictionary if you need help.

construed: _____

majority: _____

certify: _____

Name/Date _____

Amendment XII (Electoral College)

1. Where do the electors (members of the Electoral College) meet?

   _____

   _____

2. What information must be on the lists they prepare after they vote?

   _____

   _____

Name/Date _____

Amendment XII (Counting the Votes)

1. Who receives and opens the lists received from the electors?

   _____

2. Who must be present when the lists are opened?

   _____

   _____

Name/Date _____

Amendment XII (Electing the President)

What happens if no one receives a majority of electoral votes for president?

_____

_____

_____

_____

Name/Date _____

Amendment XII
(Electing the Vice President)

What happens if no one receives a majority of electoral votes for vice president?

_____

_____

_____

_____

The U.S. Constitution Warm-ups
Amendments XIII through XV

Name/Date _____

_____

Amendments XIII–XV

Write a short definition for each word. Feel free to use a dictionary.

naturalized: _____

_____

_____

immunities: _____

_____

_____

apportioned: _____

_____

_____

emancipation: _____

_____

_____

Name/Date _____

Amendment XIII, 1

In addition to freeing all slaves in the U.S. and lands claimed by the U.S., Amendment XIII also made involuntary servitude illegal, with one exception. Answer these questions on your own paper.

1. What does "involuntary servitude" mean?

2. When is involuntary servitude legal?

Name/Date _____

Amendment XIII, 2

Amendment XIII was ratified shortly after the end of the Civil War. On another sheet of paper, explain how the feelings against southerners were evident in this amendment.

END SLAVERY

Name/Date _____

Amendment XIV

Answer these questions on your own paper.
1. According to Amendment XIV, what criteria did someone have to meet to be a U.S. citizen? (Be sure to read the second paragraph before answering.)
2. Which three groups of people were not considered citizens and did not have the right to vote?
3. Amendment XIV also made it illegal to deprive citizens of what three things without due process of law?

Name/Date _____

Amendment XV

Since all former male slaves over 21 became citizens by Amendment XIV, why do you think Amendment XV was considered necessary? Write your answer on another sheet of paper.

The U.S. Constitution Warm-ups
Amendments XVI and XVII

Name/Date _____

Amendment XVI, 1

1. What power did Amendment XVI give Congress?

   _____

2. Do you think people should pay income taxes? Why or why not?

   _____

   _____

   _____

Name/Date _____

Amendment XVI, 2

For a short time during the Civil War, President Lincoln made taxes based on income legal (temporarily) to help pay for the war. How do you think you would have felt about that?

_____

_____

_____

_____

Name/Date _____

Amendment XVI, 3

Take a poll of at least 20 adults. (You could ask relatives, neighbors, and teachers.) Ask if they think income taxes are fair or unfair. Use the data you collected to make a graph.

Name/Date _____

Amendment XVI, 4

Income taxes do not provide all of the money needed to support the government. What other methods provide the government with money at the city, state, or federal level?

_____

_____

_____

_____

Name/Date _____

Amendment XVII

1. Review the first paragraph of Section 3. How did Amendment XVII change the way senators are elected? _____

2. Which way do you think is better? Why? _____

   _____

3. If a vacancy occurs in the Senate, what are the two ways the position can be filled temporarily?

   _____

   _____

The U.S. Constitution Warm-ups
Amendments XVIII and XIX

Name/Date _____

Amendment XVIII, 1

1. What was illegal according to Amendment XVIII?

   _____

   _____

2. Was it illegal to drink alcohol? _____

3. When did this law take effect?

   _____

Name/Date _____

Amendment XVIII, 2

Why do you think Amendment XVIII was very unpopular? Write your answer on another sheet of paper.

Name/Date _____

Amendments XVII–XIX

Write "F" for fact or "O" for opinion on the lines next to each statement.

1. _____ Amendment XIX gave women over 21 the right to vote.
2. _____ Making the sale of liquor illegal was a good law.
3. _____ The president and vice president should be elected by popular vote.
4. _____ Women should have had the right to vote when the Constitution was first written.
5. _____ The states had seven years to ratify Amendment XVIII.
6. _____ Income taxes are not fair.

Name/Date _____

Compare and Contrast

In general terms, compare and contrast the first ten amendments to the Constitution to Amendments XI through XIX. Use another sheet of paper.

Name/Date _____

Amendments XII–XIX

Amendment XVIII is often referred to as the "Prohibition Amendment." For each amendment listed, write a short phrase to describe it on your own paper.

Amendment XII   Amendment XIII

Amendment XV   Amendment XVI

Amendment XIX

The U.S. Constitution Warm-ups
Amendments XX and XXI

Name/Date _____

_____

Amendment XX, 1

Although presidential and congressional elections took place in November, under the original Constitution, the president and vice president did not take office until March. New members of Congress had to wait until the following December (13 months) before taking office. Those who had not been reelected were referred to as "lame ducks" from November until they took office.

Why do you think they were referred to as "lame ducks"?

_____

_____

_____

_____

_____

_____

Name/Date _____

Amendment XX, 2

1. T F Amendment XX changed the frequency of when Congress convenes.
2. T F The date the president took office was changed to January 3.
3. T F If the president-elect dies before taking office, a new election must be held.

Name/Date _____

Amendment XXI, 1

Answer the following questions on your own paper.
1. What does repeal mean?
2. Which amendment was repealed by Amendment XXI?
3. Under what circumstances was the importing or transportation of alcohol still illegal?

Name/Date _____

Amendment XXI, 2

Would you have voted for or against Amendment XXI? List three reasons for your answer.

_____

_____

_____

Name/Date _____

Amendments XX and XXI

Which amendment, XX or XXI, do you think had the most impact on American society? Write your answer on another sheet of paper. Give at least three reasons.

LIQUOR FOR SALE

The U.S. Constitution Warm-ups
Amendments XXII and XXIII

Name/Date _____

Amendment XXII, 1

1. According to Amendment XXII, how many times can a person be elected president? ___
2. If the vice president takes over for the president during the last year of the president's term, how many times could that person be elected president? ___
3. If the vice president takes over for the president during the first two years of the president's term, how many times could that person be elected president? ___

Name/Date _____

Amendment XXII, 2

At present, there are no term limits for members of Congress and many other elected positions in the U.S. Do you think all elected positions should have term limits? Why or why not? Write your answer on another sheet of paper.

If yes, how many years do you think is the most one person should hold an elected office?

Name/Date _____

Amendment XXII, 3

President Franklin Roosevelt was so popular that he was elected four times. List the pros and cons of having term limits for the president.

Pros

_____

_____

_____

_____

Cons

_____

_____

_____

_____

Name/Date _____

Amendment XXIII

People living in the nation's capital are not residents of any state. Therefore, they could not vote for the president and had no representation in Congress.

1. What is the nation's capital?

   _____

2. What limit is placed on the number of Electors for the capital? _____

   _____

Name/Date _____

Create a Venn Diagram

On another sheet of paper, draw a large Venn diagram. Use the diagram to show similarities and differences between any two amendments or ideas found in the Constitution.

The U.S. Constitution Warm-ups
Amendments XXIV through XXVI

Name/Date _____

Amendment XXIV

Amendment XXIV made it illegal to impose a poll tax on voters.

1. What is a poll tax? _____

_____

2. What could happen if a poll tax were legal? _____

_____

_____

Name/Date _____

Amendment XXV, 1

Why is it a good idea for the vice president to be able to take over temporarily if the president cannot perform his duties due to illness or other factors?

_____

_____

_____

_____

_____

Name/Date _____

Amendment XXV, 2

1. If the president is permanently unable to perform his duties for any reason, the _____ _____ becomes the president.

2. If the vice president's position is vacant for any reason, the _____ nominates someone to fill that position.

3. A _____ of both houses of Congress must agree to confirm that person as vice president.

4. If the president is temporarily unable to perform his duties, the vice president becomes

_____.

Name/Date _____

Amendment XXVI, 1

Circle "F" for fact or "O" for opinion.

1. F O 18-year-old citizens of the United States are eligible to vote.

2. F O The voting age should be dropped to 16.

3. F O 18-year-olds are mature enough to vote.

Name/Date _____

Amendment XXVI, 2

Amendment XXVI changed the voting age from 21 to 18. Do you think people who are under 21 should be allowed to vote? Why or why not?

_____

_____

_____

_____

_____

The U.S. Constitution Warm-ups
Amendment XXVII and Review

Name/Date _____

Amendment XXVII

1. Who approves salary increases for members of Congress?

   _____

2. What limit does Amendment XXVII put on salary changes for members of Congress?

   _____

   _____

   _____

Name/Date _____

Salaries

Use reference sources. What is the current annual salary for each position?

_____ President

_____ Vice President

_____ Senator

_____ Member of the House of Representatives

_____ Your favorite athlete

Name/Date _____

Write the Questions

For each answer, write a question on your own paper.

Answers

1. the Constitution
2. the president
3. a right of a citizen
4. executive, legislative, and judicial

Name/Date _____

Branch Scramble

Unscramble the letters below to form the words for the three branches of our federal government.

1. DIIJLAUC   _____

2. TEXVECIUE   _____

3. ATLISVEGLIE   _____

Name/Date _____

Review Amendments XX–XXVII

Write the number of the amendment for each phrase. Feel free to go back and review the Constitution to find the answers.

1. _____ Granted Washington, D.C., electoral votes

2. _____ Abolished the poll tax

3. _____ Changed dates president and members of Congress take office

4. _____ Lowered voting age to 18

5. _____ Limits term of the president

6. _____ Repealed prohibition

7. _____ Provided for temporarily covering the president's incapacity to hold office

---

The U.S. Constitution Warm-ups
What Do You Think?

Name/Date _____

What Do You Think? 1

In the early days, most people thought the position of vice president was not very important. What do you think? Write your answer on your own paper.

VICE PRESIDENT

Name/Date _____

What Do You Think? 2

The Constitution has been called the "most important document ever written." What do you think? Write your answer on your own paper.

Name/Date _____

What Do You Think? 3

Some people claim that it costs so much to run a campaign for a major office that only those who are rich can be elected. What do you think? Write your answer on your own paper.

$50 $10 $50 $20 $100 $20

Name/Date _____

What Do You Think? 4

During campaigns, candidates often inform the public of negative things about their opponents, including information that may be very private and personal. Does the public have the right to know everything about a candidate? Do people running for office have any rights to privacy? What do you think? Write your answer on your own paper.

Name/Date _____

_____

What Do You Think? 5

At the time this book was written, no woman or African-American had been elected president or vice president. Why do you think it has taken so long for someone from either of these groups to be elected to one of the nation's top two positions? Continue your answer on another sheet of paper if you need more room to write.

_____

_____

_____

_____

_____

_____

_____

_____

_____

_____

_____

_____

_____

Answer Keys

The Preamble 1 (p. 20)
preamble: an introduction
domestic: of one's own home or country
tranquility: peace
posterity: all of a person's descendants
ordain: to decree or order

The Preamble 2 (p. 20)
To form a more perfect Union, establish Justice, insure domestic Tranquility, provide for the common defence, promote the general Welfare, and secure the Blessings of Liberty to ourselves and our Posterity (any three)

The Preamble 3 (p. 20)
defence (defense)
The words are important nouns in the sentence.

Congress 1 (p. 21)
legislative: having the power to make laws
requisite: required; necessary
enumeration: a count; list
subsequent: coming after; following in time, place, or order

Congress 2 (p. 21)
Representatives must be at least 25 years old, a citizen of the U.S. for 7 years, and a resident of the state from which he or she is elected.

Congress 4 (p. 21)
1. 2 years
2. Speaker of the House
3. Members of the House of Representatives

Congress 6 (p. 22)
1. The Senate and the House of Representatives
2. Two
3. 6 years
4. The vice president

Congress 7 (p. 22)
pro tempore: temporary
impeachment: the act of bringing a public official before the proper tribunal on charges of wrongdoing
affirmation: a solemn declaration, but not under oath

concurrence: agreement; accord
liable: legally bound or obligated; responsible

Congress 8 (p. 22)
Senators must be at least 30 years old, a citizen of the U.S. for at least 9 years, and a resident of the state from which he or she is elected.

Congress 13 (p. 23)
adjourn: to close a session or meeting for a time
quorum: minimum number of members that must be present to do business
revenue: income from taxes, licenses, etc.
veto: to prevent a bill from becoming law by refusing to sign it

Congress 15 (p. 23)
A bill is a proposed law not yet approved by both Houses of Congress and the President.

Congress 18 (p. 24)
See Article 1: Section 8 for list.

Congress 19 (p. 24)
See Article 1: Section 9 for list.

The President 1 (p. 25)
executive: empowered and required to administer; administrative
emolument: gain from employment or position; salary, fees, etc.
reprieve: to postpone the punishment of
militia: an army composed of citizens rather than professional soldiers

The President 2 (p. 25)
1. T 2. F 3. F 4. F

The President 6 (p. 26)
1. The president must be at least 35 years old, a natural-born citizen of the U.S., and a resident of the U.S. for at least 14 years.
2. See Article 2: Section 2 for list.

The President 10 (p. 26)
Congress might vote to pay a popular president more or an unpopular president less.

The President 11 (p. 27)
1. The President can be removed from office if impeached and convicted of treason, bribery, or high crimes and misdemeanors.

The Judicial Branch 1 (p. 28)
judicial: of judges or law courts
inferior: lower in order, status, or rank
jurisdiction: the authority or legal power to hear and decide cases
appellate: having jurisdiction to review appeals

The Judicial Branch 2 (p. 28)
1. ambassadors
2. treason
3. lower (reduce)
4. Congress

The States 1 (p. 29)
1. T   2. F   3. T   4. T   5. F

The States 2 (p. 29)
If a person commits a crime in one state and flees to another state, he or she can legally be returned to the state where the crime was committed.

Amending the Constitution 1 (p. 29)
1. Two-thirds of both houses
2. approved
3. three-fourths

Upholding the Constitution (p. 29)
All members of Congress, members of state legislatures, and federal and state officers of the executive and judicial departments must promise to uphold the Constitution.

Review 1 (p. 30)
1. 4 years   2. 4 years   3. 6 years
4. 2 years   5. none specified   6. life

Review 2 (p. 30)
1. E   2. E   3. J   4. L   5. J
6. L

Review 3 (p. 30)
1. 30   2. 35   3. 35   4. none specified
5. none specified   6. 25

Review 4 (p. 30)
1. Nine   2. June 21, 1788

Review 5 (p. 30)
1. Y   2. N   3. Y   4. N   5. Y
6. N   7. Y   8. Y   9. N   10. N

The Bill of Rights 1 (p. 32)
Freedom of religion, speech, press, assembly, and petition

The Bill of Rights 3 (p. 32)
abridge: to reduce or lessen
quartered: provided with lodgings
seizure: the act of arresting or confiscating
indictment: a formal written accusation charging someone of a crime

The Bill of Rights 5 (p. 32)
1. IV   2. II   3. V   4. III   5. V

The Bill of Rights 6 (p. 33)
1. Weapons

The Bill of Rights 8 (p. 33)
1. taken without permission
2. There must be probable cause for the search. In addition, a legal search warrant must be issued describing the place to be searched and the persons or things to be seized.

The Bill of Rights 9 (p. 33)
1. The right not to be a witness against oneself in court.

The Bill of Rights 11 (p. 34)
1. Y   2. N   3. N   4. Y   5. Y
6. N

The Bill of Rights 12 (p. 34)
1. VI   2. VIII   3. VI   4. VI   5. VIII

Amendment XI and XII (p. 35)
construed: explained or deduced the meaning of
majority: more than half of a total
certify: to declare true, accurate, or certain

Amendment XII (Electoral College) (p. 35)
1. in their respective states
2. names of everyone who received votes for president and vice president and the number of votes each one received

Amendment XII (Counting the Votes) (p. 35)
1. The President of the Senate
2. Members of the Senate and House of Representatives

Amendment XII (Electing the President) (p. 35)

If no one received a majority of electoral votes for president, members of the House of Representatives vote for one of the top three candidates.

Amendment XII (Electing the Vice President) (p. 35)

If no one received a majority of electoral votes for vice president, members of the Senate vote for one of the top two candidates.

Amendment XIII–XV (p. 36)

naturalized: to have had citizenship granted to one who was not a native-born citizen

immunities: exemptions or freedoms

apportioned: divided or distributed according to a plan

emancipation: the act of setting free

Amendment XIII, 1 (p. 36)

1. Being forced to work for someone else against your will
2. When it is punishment for a crime

Amendment XIV (p. 36)

1. Citizens were males over 21 who were born or naturalized in the United States.
2. People under 21, Native Americans, and women
3. Life, liberty, or property

Amendment XVI, 1 (p. 37)

1. The power to impose taxes based on income

Amendment XVII (p. 37)

1. Senators are now elected by popular vote rather than by the state legislatures.
3. The governor of the state can appoint someone to serve until the next regular election or call for a special election.

Amendment XVIII, 1 (p. 38)

1. Manufacture, sale, and transportation of alcoholic beverages in the United States
2. No. That is not specified.
3. January 16, 1920 (One year after the Amendment was ratified.)

Amendments XVII through XIX (p. 38)

1. F   2. O   3. O   4. O   5. F
6. O

Amendments XII–XIX (p. 38)

Amendment XII: Electing president and vice president

Amendment XIII: Abolishing slavery

Amendment XV: Former slaves can vote

Amendment XVI: Legalized income taxes

Amendment XIX: Women can vote

Amendment XX, 2 (p. 39)

1. F   2. F   3. F

Amendment XXI, 1 (p. 39)

1. revoke, cancel
2. Amendment XVIII
3. It remained illegal in "dry" states, ones that chose to make alcohol illegal even after prohibition had been repealed.

Amendment XXII, 1 (p. 40)

1. 2   2. 2   3. 1

Amendment XXIII (p. 40)

1. Washington, D.C. (the District of Columbia)
2. Residents may not have more electors than the number held by the least populous state.

Amendment XXIV (p. 41)

1. A tax paid in order to vote
2. People who could not afford to pay the tax would not be able to vote.

Amendment XXV, 2 (p. 41)

1. vice president   2. president
3. majority   4. acting president

Amendment XXVI, 1 (p. 41)

1. F   2. O   3. O

Amendment XXVII (p. 42)

1. Congress
2. Pay changes do not take affect until after the next election of members of the House of Representatives

Branch Scramble (p. 42)

1. JUDICIAL   2. EXECUTIVE
3. LEGISLATIVE

Review Amendments XX through XXVII (p. 42)

1. XXIII   2. XXIV   3. XX
4. XXVI   5. XXII   6. XXI
7. XXV